SAFE SPACES

SAFE SPACES

Making Schools and Communities Welcoming to LGBT Youth

Annemarie Vaccaro, Gerri August, and Megan S. Kennedy

Foreword by Barbara M. Newman

 PRAEGER

AN IMPRINT OF ABC-CLIO, LLC
Santa Barbara, California • Denver, Colorado • Oxford, England

Library of Congress Cataloging-in-Publication Data

Vaccaro, Annemarie.

  Safe spaces : making schools and communities welcoming to LGBT youth / Annemarie Vaccaro, Gerri August, and Megan S. Kennedy ; foreword by Barbara M. Newman.

    p. cm.

  Includes bibliographical references and index.

  ISBN 978–0–313–39368–6 (hardback : acid-free paper) — ISBN 978–0–313–39369–3 (ebook)

1. Sexual minority youth—United States. 2. Sexual minority youth—Psychology—United States. 3. Sexual minority youth—Education—United States. 4. Public schools—Social aspects—United States. I. August, Gerri. II. Kennedy, Megan S. III. Title.

HQ76.27.Y68V33   2012

306.76′608350973—dc23   2011033278

ISBN: 978–0–313–39368–6
EISBN: 978–0–313–39369–3

16 15 14 13 12   2 3 4 5

This book is also available on the World Wide Web as an eBook.
Visit www.abc-clio.com for details.

Praeger
An Imprint of ABC-CLIO, LLC

ABC-CLIO, LLC
130 Cremona Drive, P.O. Box 1911
Santa Barbara, California 93116-1911

This book is printed on acid-free paper ∞

Manufactured in the United States of America

We dedicate this book to LGBT youth who persevere, and even thrive, despite sometimes overwhelming tides of homophobia, transphobia, genderism, and heterosexism. We also salute youth and adult allies who work tirelessly to make our schools and communities safe spaces.